Exploring
CALIFORNIA
MISSIONS

SAN FRANCISCO BAY AREA MISSIONS

❖

BY
TEKLA N. WHITE

❖

CONSULTANT:
JAMES J. RAWLS, PhD
PROFESSOR EMERITUS
DEPARTMENT OF HISTORY
DIABLO VALLEY COLLEGE

LERNER PUBLICATIONS COMPANY/MINNEAPOLIS

The images in this book are used with the permission of: © North Wind Picture Archives, pp. 6, 44; © Westend 61/Alamy, p. 8; Courtesy of the Bancroft Library, University of California, Berkeley, pp. 12, 13 (right), 14, 21, 29, 39, 40; © Frank S. Balthis, p. 13 (left); © Lake County Museum/CORBIS, p. 15; The Granger Collection, New York, pp. 16, 24, 36; © Ron Bohr, pp. 18, 31, 48, 53; Zephyrin Engelhardt, *The Missions and Missionaries of California, 1908-1915*, pp. 20, 22, 43; © Diana Petersen, pp. 23, 25, 33, 50 (both), 51, 52, 54, 55; © Bettmann/CORBIS, p. 27; Collection of Oakland Museum of California, Museum of Donors' Acquisition Fund, p. 28; © Michael T. Sedam/CORBIS, p. 30; © Robert Holmes/CORBIS, p. 32; © Dr. Sylvan H. Wittwer/Visuals Unlimited, p. 34; Santa Clara University, p. 41; The Huntington Library, San Marino, CA, p. 42; Seaver Center for Western History, Los Angeles County Museum of Natural History, p. 46; © Lynda Richards, p. 49; maps and diagrams on pp. 4, 11, 26, 57, 58, 59 by © Laura Westlund/Independent Picture Service.

Front cover: © Diana Petersen
Back cover: © Laura Westlund/Independent Picture Service

Lerner Publications Company
A division of Lerner Publishing Group, Inc.
241 First Avenue North
Minneapolis, MN 55401 U.S.A.

Website address: www.lernerbooks.com

Library of Congress Cataloging-in-Publication Data

White, Tekla N.
    San Francisco Bay area missions / by Tekla White.
        p.   cm. — (Exploring california missions)
    Includes index.
    ISBN 978–0–8225–0900–4 (lib. bdg. : alk. paper)
        1. Missions, Spanish—California—San Francisco Bay Area—History—Juvenile literature. 2. San Francisco Bay Area (Calif.)—History—Juvenile literature. 3. Indians of North America—Missions—California—San Francisco Bay Area—Juvenile literature. 4. Spanish mission buildings—California—San Francisco Bay Area—Juvenile literature. I. Title.
    F868.S156W44 2008
    979.4'6—dc22   2006036846

Manufactured in the United States of America
1 2 3 4 5 6 – DP – 13 12 11 10 09 08

CONTENTS

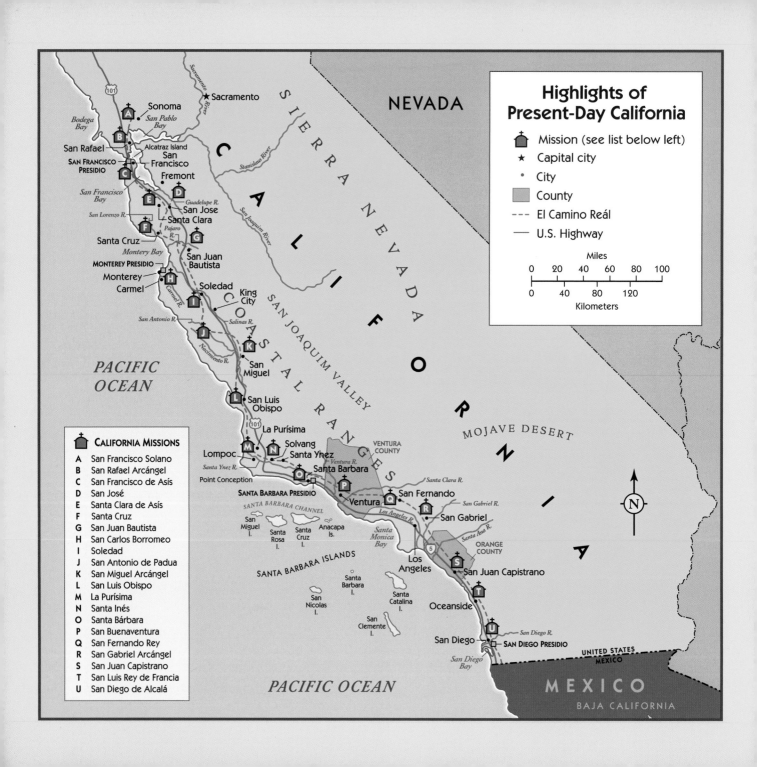

INTRODUCTION

Spain and the Roman Catholic Church built twenty California **missions** between 1769 and 1817. A final mission was built in 1823. The missions stand along a narrow strip of California's Pacific coast. Today, the missions sit near Highway 101. They are between the cities of San Diego and Sonoma.

The Spaniards built **presidios** (forts) and missions throughout their empire. This system helped the Spanish claim and protect new lands. In California, the main goal of the mission system was to control Native Americans and their lands. The Spaniards wanted Native Americans to accept their leadership and way of life.

Spanish **missionaries** and soldiers ran the presidio and mission system. Father Junípero Serra was the missions' first leader. He was called father-president. Father Serra and the other priests taught Native Americans the Catholic faith. The priests showed them how to behave like Spaniards. The soldiers made sure Native Americans obeyed the priests.

The area was home to many Native American groups. They had their own beliefs and practices. The Spanish ways were much different from their own. Some Native Americans willingly joined the missions. But others did not. They did not want to give up their own ways of life.

The Spaniards tried different methods to make Native Americans join their missions. Sometimes they gave the Native Americans gifts. Other times, the Spanish used force. To stay alive, the Native Americans had no choice but to join the missions.

The Spanish called Native Americans who joined their missions **neophytes**. The Spaniards taught neophytes the Catholic religion. The neophytes built buildings and farmed the land. They also produced goods, such as cloth and soap. They built a trade route connecting the missions. It was called El Camino Reál (the Royal Road). The goods and trade were expected to earn money and power for Spain.

A Spanish missionary instructs Native Americans.

But the system did not last. More than half of the Native Americans died from diseases the Spaniards brought. Mexico took control of the area in 1821 and closed the missions. Neophytes were free to leave or stay at the missions. In 1848, the United States gained control of California. Some of the remaining neophytes returned to their people. But many others had no people to return to. They moved to **pueblos** (towns) or inland areas. The missions sat empty. They fell apart over time.

This book is about the five missions in the San Francisco Bay area. Spanish missionaries founded San Francisco de Asís in 1776, Santa Clara de Asís in 1777, and Mission San José in 1797. They set up San Rafael Arcángel as a hospital in 1817. San Francisco Solano was established in 1823.

CALIFORNIA MISSION	FOUNDING DATE
San Diego de Alcalá	July 16, 1769
San Carlos Borromeo de Carmelo	June 3, 1770
San Antonio de Padua	July 14, 1771
San Gabriel Arcángel	September 8, 1771
San Luis Obispo de Tolosa	September 1, 1772
San Francisco de Asís	June 29, 1776
San Juan Capistrano	November 1, 1776
Santa Clara de Asís	January 12, 1777
San Buenaventura	March 31, 1782
Santa Bárbara Virgen y Mártir	December 4, 1786
La Purísima Concepción de Maria Santísima	December 8, 1787
Santa Cruz	August 28, 1791
Nuestra Señora de la Soledad	October 9, 1791
San José	June 11, 1797
San Juan Bautista	June 24, 1797
San Miguel Arcángel	July 25, 1797
San Fernando Rey de España	September 8, 1797
San Luis Rey de Francia	June 13, 1798
Santa Inés Virgen y Mártir	September 17, 1804
San Rafael Arcángel	December 14, 1817
San Francisco Solano	July 4, 1823

The California coast
near San Francisco

·1·

EARLY LIFE IN THE BAY AREA

The San Francisco Bay area is the home of modern cities. But, in many ways, the area appears as it did long ago. The Pacific Ocean washes into the bay and onto sandy shores and rocky cliff walls. Hills rise to the east. The climate is warm but damp and rainy. The rains fill streams, and rivers and springs form ponds. The waterways meet the sea in wet areas called marshes.

In earlier times, woods of willow, pine, and oak stood along the coast. Many kinds of wildlife, fish, and plants lived in the area. Geese and ducks stopped and fed in the marshes. Rabbits, deer, and bears roamed the hills. The bay was full of fish and shellfish. Salmon swam in the rivers. The oaks and pines were plentiful with acorns and pine nuts. **Tule** grew in the marshes. Berries filled the woods.

NATIVE AMERICANS

The San Francisco Bay area is the homeland of two Native American groups. The Ohlone and the Coast Miwok have lived in the Bay Area for thousands of years. In early times, the Ohlone lived south of the bay along the Pacific Ocean. The Coast Miwok lived to the north.

The land provided all that they needed. The Ohlone trapped ducks and geese in the marshes and gathered shellfish along the coast. The Coast Miwok netted salmon and eel in the rivers. In the summer, both groups hunted deer, rabbits, and other animals. They gathered nuts, berries, and plants. Acorns were most important. The Coast Miwok and Ohlone used acorns to make flour for soft cereal and breads. They wove tule to make homes, canoes, and clothing.

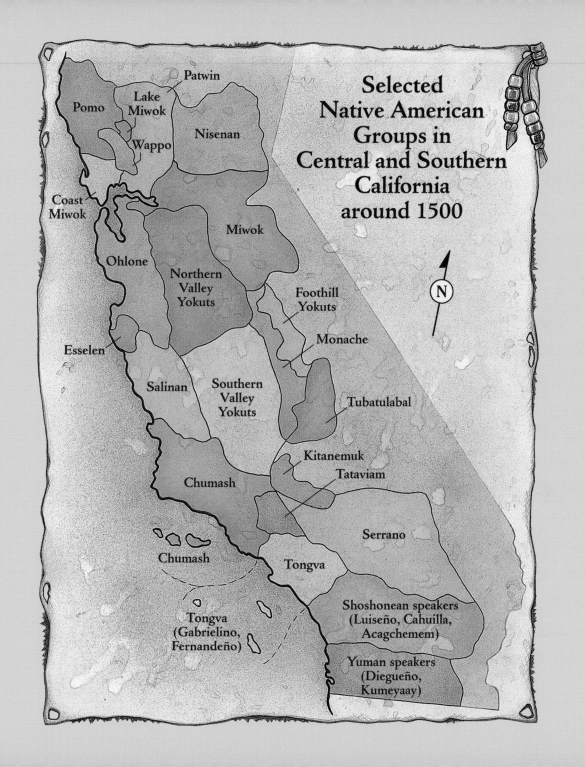

Selected
Native American
Groups in
Central and Southern
California
around 1500

N

Patwin
Lake Miwok
Pomo
Nisenan
Wappo
Coast Miwok
Miwok
Ohlone
Northern Valley Yokuts
Foothill Yokuts
Monache
Esselen
Salinan
Southern Valley Yokuts
Tubatulabal
Kitanemuk
Tataviam
Chumash
Serrano
Chumash
Tongva
Shoshonean speakers
(Luiseño, Cahuilla,
Acagchemem)
Tongva
(Gabrielino,
Fernandeño)
Yuman speakers
(Diegueño,
Kumeyaay)

The Coast Miwok and the Ohlone wore clothing that suited the warm climate. Women wore skirts woven from tule. Men often wore only belts to hold tools. When it was cold, they covered themselves with cloaks made of rabbit skins.

The Ohlone and the Coast Miwok had their own way of living and their own languages and religion. The Ohlone people spoke eight different languages. In their society, a tribal leader ruled over a small grouping of Ohlone villages. Storytellers taught young Ohlone children tribal beliefs.

The Coast Miwok were expert fishers, netting fish from tule canoes or spearing them in shallow waters.

The Coast Miwok traded goods with other tribes. They made long canoes from bundled, dry tule. They created woven baskets that could hold water. The Coast Miwok celebrated the acorn harvest and other special occasions with dances and songs.

The Coast Miwok and the Ohlone shared a respect for the land. They saw that the land was the source of life. They gathered from it only what met their needs. Each understood that the group had to work together to survive.

The Ohlone gathered acorns in the fall. California Indians often kept them in large storehouses (*right*).

Sir Francis Drake probably met Coast Miwok when he landed near the Bay Area in 1579.

NEWCOMERS

Spanish and English explorers came ashore at **Alta California** in the late 1500s. English captain Sir Francis Drake landed near the San Francisco Bay area. He traded with a group of American Indians, probably the Coast Miwok. Drake claimed the area for England. The Spanish sent explorers from the south. They claimed the area for Spain. Then England and Spain seemed to forget about the area.

Father Serra founded the first mission in San Diego in 1769.

In the mid-1700s, Spanish king Carlos III decided the land should be protected for Spain. He ordered explorers, soldiers, and missionaries to the new land. Once there, they were to create settlements and start farming. The Spaniards planned ways to make the American Indians living there follow the Spanish and become workers. They also planned to teach the American Indians about the Catholic faith.

Missions seemed the best way to do this. Father Junípero Serra led the mission plan. Beginning in San Diego, Father Serra was to build missions as far north as what would become Monterey. If the plan worked, these missions would one day become Spanish pueblos.

The large San Francisco Bay appealed to explorers searching for locations for new settlements.

The first mission was established in San Diego, far south of the Bay Area. About the same time, Captain Gaspar de Portolá led an expedition north. He came upon the San Francisco Bay area. He along with later Spanish explorers sent reports about the area. The Spanish explorers said that the Bay Area would be a good place for a new mission.

THE ANZA EXPEDITION

In late 1775, a group of soldiers, priests, and settlers left Spanish settlements south of Alta California. Captain Juan Bautista de Anza led the group north. They traveled by land and reached the mission near Monterey Bay in March 1776. Anza left to find a good location for the new mission.

Anza chose the San Francisco Bay area. In June 1776, a Spanish officer named José Moraga led the settlers to the area. They set up a pueblo called Yerba Buena in what is now San Francisco. A Spanish supply ship sailed into San Francisco Bay nearly two months later. The settlers began building.

The settlers worked quickly. By mid-September, they had made buildings using clay bricks called **adobe**. On October 9, 1776, Father Francisco Palóu said Mass in the new mission church. Mission San Francisco de Asís officially became the sixth mission in Alta California.

San José mission and cemetery in modern day

·2·

MISSIONS OF THE SAN FRANCISCO BAY AREA

Each mission in the San Francisco Bay area has its own history. San Francisco de Asís had difficulty gaining and keeping neophytes. But Santa Clara de Asís was home to many neophytes. It was the most productive of all the missions.

San José faced serious problems. Local native peoples and some neophytes fought against the mission and Spanish soldiers. San Rafael Arcángel first served as a hospital before becoming a mission. San Francisco Solano was the only mission built after Spain lost control of Alta California.

A priest directs the work of neophytes. American Indians helped build all the California missions.

MISSION SAN FRANCISCO DE ASÍS

San Francisco de Asís was in the Ohlone homeland. But from 1776 to 1777, the Spanish could not get any Ohlone to join the mission. Priests and settlers worked to improve San Francisco de Asís. They built a chapel and other buildings around four sides of an open, rectangular patio. This building plan is called a **quadrangle**.

By the late 1700s, the priests had convinced many Ohlone to join the mission. The population was highest during this time. To make room, the neophytes and priests tore down the old mission. They built a new quadrangle. It had a larger church, workshops, living quarters, and storage.

Daily life at the mission was like life at other missions in Alta California. The missionaries and neophytes kept a strict daily schedule. The ringing of bells marked the different parts of the day. Bells at sunrise called people to morning church services. Neophytes learned the Catholic religion during services. Bells called the neophytes back to work and to meals. They signaled the end of the day.

San Francisco de Asís is also called Mission Dolores. Its adobe church was finished in 1791.

American Indians were the main workforce at the missions. They did not receive pay for their work.

Work at the missions was hard. Neophytes worked all day. Some made adobe bricks and constructed the mission's buildings. They also prepared meals and made clothing. Many neophytes worked in the fields. They plowed, sowed grains, planted fruit trees, and harvested crops. Other neophytes worked with livestock. They tended horses, mules, and herds of cattle and sheep.

San Francisco de Asís did well for a few years. The neophytes raised many crops and made goods. But the Ohlone did not want to stay at the mission. They missed their people and old way of life. Sicknesses such as the measles and **smallpox** killed many Ohlone at the missions. Eventually soldiers had to bring neophytes from other missions to keep San Francisco de Asís running.

A statue of Santa Clara stands in the mission.

MISSION SANTA CLARA DE ASÍS

On January 6, 1777, a group left Mission San Francisco de Asís. Led by José Moraga, the group of priests and soldiers traveled south to set up a new mission. They went through Ohlone lands. They reached the Guadalupe River. Father Tómas de la Peña placed a cross in the ground near the river. On January 12, he held the first Mass at Mission Santa Clara de Asís. Other priests arrived a few days later.

Few Ohlone wanted to join the new mission. The priests and other men built a few mission buildings. The priests farmed small fields to grow crops for their own needs. But they had to rely on other missions for supplies.

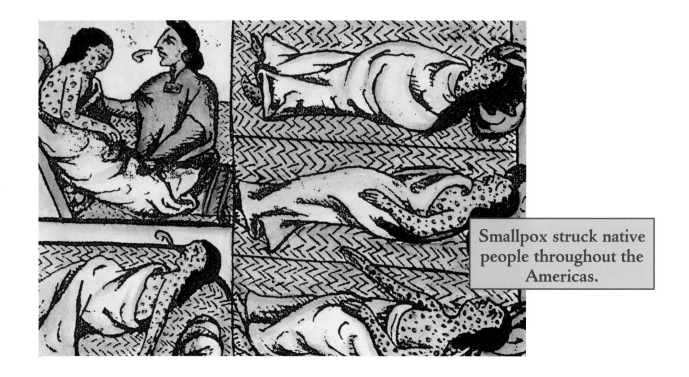

Smallpox struck native people throughout the Americas.

In the late 1700s, a sickness struck the Ohlone. The priests went to the Ohlone villages and tended to many sick children. They baptized many Ohlone. Some got well. The priests and soldiers took the baptized children back to the mission. Ohlone parents followed them. In time, many other Ohlone became neophytes. But periods of great illness remained a problem at all the missions in the San Francisco Bay area.

By the early 1800s, Santa Clara de Asís was flourishing. It grew more crops than it needed. Neophytes produced many goods. The mission supplied the presidio at San Francisco. Settlers in the pueblo of San José de Guadalupe traded for mission goods.

But the soldiers and the settlers were not happy. They did not like it that the mission had workers and good farmland. The settlers and mission priests could not agree on how to share grazing land for their animals or water from the Guadalupe River. The head priest offered a sign of peace. He had a road built joining the pueblo and the mission. But few townspeople ever visited the mission.

The area around Santa Clara de Asís and San José held good grazing lands.

Highlights of the San Francisco Bay Area, Early 1800s

MISSION SAN JOSÉ

In 1785, Father Fermín Francisco de Lasuén became the leader of all the missions in Alta California. He founded Mission San José in June 1797. He chose an area along the Guadalupe River. The area was northeast of pueblo San José Guadalupe. San José became the fourteenth mission.

Construction of the quadrangle began right away.

Soldiers and neophytes from Santa Clara de Asís built housing. They set up a church. It was to stand only a few years until the final one could be built. Priests at Santa Clara de Asís sent livestock and supplies to the new mission. Thirty-three neophytes joined the mission the first year.

In 1806, new mission leaders came to San José. The priests oversaw the completion of a new church. They brought American Indians to the mission and made them neophytes. With the neophytes' work, the mission soon produced many crops and goods.

Mission San José
around 1830

But there were many difficulties too. Neophytes became ill and died. The priests did not know the local languages. And the neophytes did not understand the Spanish language and religion. Many neophytes chose not to adapt to the Spanish way of life. They often ran away from the mission.

In 1828, a neophyte named Estanislao left Mission San José to visit his family. He decided not to return to the mission. Estanislao was angry at the Spanish for taking his people's

A man performs a ceremonial Ohlone dance. Many Ohlone did not want to leave their traditions for life in the missions.

and other American Indians' lands. He did not think it was right to force American Indians to work at the missions.

He gathered a group of neophytes from San José and other missions to fight the Spanish. Other Native Americans joined his group. They fought the Spanish for one year. Many of Estanislao's followers were killed. In 1829, Spanish soldiers attacked Estanislao's camp and trapped him. He gave up his fight and returned to Mission San José. Estanislao died of smallpox there many years later.

Troops from the San Francisco presidio helped control Native Americans in the Bay Area.

MISSION SAN RAFAEL ARCÁNGEL

In 1812, Russia built Fort Ross north of San Francisco Bay. Spanish leaders feared that Russia would take over the area. The governor of Alta California said that the missionaries of San Francisco de Asís should claim lands across the bay. In December of 1817, a group of Spanish soldiers and priests sailed across the bay. They chose an area for a small hospital.

Fort Ross was the center of the Russian colony in Alta California.

Set up as a hospital, San Rafael Arcángel also had a church.

Neophytes from San Francisco de Asís built the small hospital and housing. The priests named the hospital San Rafael Arcángel after the angel of healing. The hospital sat on the Coast Miwok homeland. But at first, few American Indians came to San Rafael.

The priests at San Francisco de Asís sent sick neophytes to the hospital. They seemed to get better there. Fewer neophytes died at San Rafael Arcángel than at the missions. Some stayed to live and work at the hospital.

In 1819, Father Juan Amorós came to run the hospital. He worked hard to better San Rafael. He brought Coast Miwok and other American Indians to live and work there. He had the land around the hospital farmed. Soon San Rafael had orchards, vineyards, and fields of grain. By 1823, seven hundred neophytes lived at the hospital. San Rafael Arcángel became Alta California's twentieth mission that year.

San Rafael Arcángel
in present day

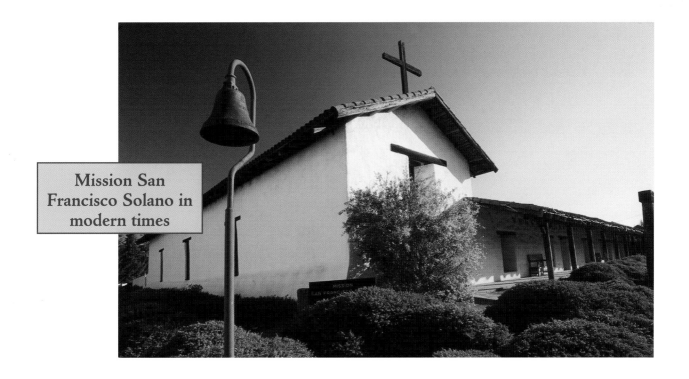

Mission San Francisco Solano in modern times

MISSION SAN FRANCISCO SOLANO

In 1823, a young priest named José Altimira received permission to found a new mission. On July 4, 1823, he claimed an area north and east of San Rafael Arcángel. The site was part of Coast Miwok lands near San Pablo Bay. In 1824, work began on a chapel for the new mission. On April 4, Father Altimira held the first Mass at San Francisco Solano. It became the twenty-first and last mission.

By this time, many Coast Miwok and other American Indians had lost their lands to the missions and settlers. They had little choice but to join the mission. San Francisco Solano flourished from the work of the neophytes. By the end of 1824, the mission had many adobe buildings. Some held areas for living and working. Others were for storing grain. Workers planted 160 fruit trees. The neophytes planted and harvested wheat fields and tended livestock.

Olive trees were cultivated at the mission.

But Father Altimira was not a good leader. He treated the neophytes very badly. American Indians in the area became angry with the priest. In 1826, they attacked the mission.

Father Altimira fled. Many neophytes also left. Other priests came to lead the mission, and the fighting was put down. Thirty new buildings were added to the mission, including an adobe church. But some of the priests were no better than Father Altimira. And time was quickly bringing the mission system to an end.

San Francisco Bay
around 1846

STATE CONTROL OF THE MISSIONS

The early 1800s was a time of trouble for Spain and its missions. Spain was fighting a war in Europe. It could not support its soldiers or settlers in Alta California.

But the missions were doing well. The soldiers and settlers soon became angry that priests controlled the missions. The soldiers and settlers wanted the mission lands for themselves.

MEXICO TAKES CONTROL

In 1821, Mexico gained its freedom from Spain. Mexico claimed the territory of California. It created laws that gave greater freedom to many. This included American Indians.

Spanish and non-Spanish settlers joined together. They called themselves **Californios.** Californios saw that they could take control of mission lands. They pleaded with the Mexican government to **secularize** the missions. This policy would put the mission lands under state, or government, control. Then the missions' land could be divided up and given to Californios.

The missionaries fought the secularization plan but lost. The Mexican government put the mission lands in control of local leaders. The government slowly replaced the missionaries with Mexican priests.

CIVIL ADMINISTRATORS AT THE MISSIONS

The Mexican government named civil administrators. These leaders were each in charge of one mission's lands. They were to make sure mission lands were divided fairly.

Without workers, San Francisco de Asís soon fell into disrepair.

They were to give some land and supplies to neophytes. But administrators often kept land for themselves. They also gave mission land to family, friends, and men in power.

In 1833, the Mexican government started its plan of secularization. Priests turned over Mission San Francisco de Asís in 1834. Only 150 neophytes lived there. Smallpox killed the remaining neophytes in 1838. Without workers, the mission buildings began to fall apart. The administrator sold or rented some of the buildings.

San Francisco Solano was secularized in 1834. The governor made General Mariano Guadalupe Vallejo the administrator. He gave Vallejo a big piece of the mission's land. Vallejo set up a large **rancho** for himself. Soon he was in charge of the entire area. The neophytes did not get any land. But General Vallejo let them work and tend cattle on his great rancho. Californios tore the mission's buildings apart for their adobe, tiles, and wood.

General Vallejo sits in front of his home in Sonoma in the late 1800s.

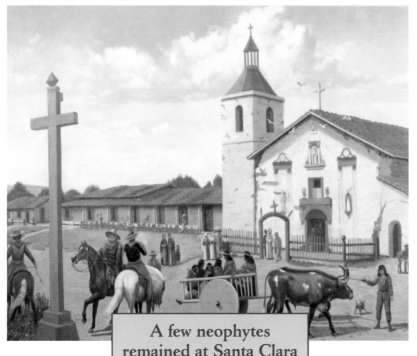

A few neophytes remained at Santa Clara after the state took over the mission's lands.

Mission San Rafael Arcángel was secularized in 1835. The mission administrator gave the neophytes their choice of livestock and lands. But General Vallejo said the neophytes misused the land. He claimed it for himself. The neophytes had no place else to go. Many of them decided to work for the general or other Californios. The neophytes received little or no pay for their work on the ranchos.

By 1836, secularization of Mission Santa Clara was under way. At this time, only about three hundred neophytes still remained at the mission. Farming and other mission work practically stopped. Californios and Native Americans in the area had stolen many mission cattle and sheep. Mexican soldiers lived in mission buildings.

Father José Reál tried to save the mission. He charged settlers rent to farm the remaining mission land. The neophytes never received any land.

Mission San José was secularized in 1836. General Vallejo's older brother, José de Jesus Vallejo, became the administrator. Mexican officials accused him of stealing and had him replaced. More than 1,300 neophytes left the mission during this time. Buildings stood empty, and thieves stole valuables from the mission.

Pío Pico gained a large amount of land that had once belonged to the missions.

In 1845, an administrator named Pío Pico became governor of the territory. He decided that all the missions should be sold or rented. He ordered all the missions to be closed. In 1846, Governor Pico sold Santa Clara's fruit orchards. He sold most of Mission San José to his brother, who was a former governor.

U.S. TAKEOVER

In the early 1840s, the United States offered to buy Alta California. But the Mexican government refused the offer. The two countries argued over the area and about other land along their borders. In 1846, the United States went to war with Mexico.

The U.S. flag is raised over Monterey Bay after the U.S. Navy took over the area in 1846.

When gold was discovered in California in 1848, many rushed to the state in hopes of striking it rich.

Mexico lost the war in 1848. The U.S. government took control of the territory. The territory became the state of California two years later. Many people from the eastern United States moved to California. The people wanted land to live on and farm. In the early 1850s, the U.S. government passed new laws. The laws said that anyone who received land from the Mexican government had to prove that the land was theirs. They had to go to court and convince officials that their land really belonged to them.

The Californios tried to prove ownership, but many failed. Most of these lands ended up in the hands of easterners. Neophytes often were never told about the laws. In time, the U.S. government moved many Califonia Indians to lands set aside for them. But these **reservations** were often on land that was not good for hunting or farming.

The new U.S. settlers cared little for the mission grounds and buildings. Most were not used. The U.S. government returned the missions to the Roman Catholic Church. During the 1850s and the 1860s, priests tried to repair the missions. But they were not able to completely restore them. It seemed that no one could save the missions.

Edwin Deakin painted San Francisco de Asís in the late 1800s. His paintings renewed interest in the California missions.

·4·

THE MISSIONS IN MODERN TIMES

In the late 1800s, stories about the missions became popular. Helen Hunt Jackson's book *Ramona* tells a story about American Indians at the missions. Guadalupe Vallejo's magazine articles share what she remembered of life at Mission San José. Readers enjoyed the stories. People began to think that the missions should be saved.

In 1895, the Landmarks Club was founded, and the California Historical Landmarks League soon followed. These groups raised money to help repair the missions.

MISSION SAN FRANCISCO DE ASÍS

San Francisco grew quickly during the gold rush of the late 1840s and 1850s. The city soon reached Mission San Francisco de Asís. As the city grew, city officials tore down mission buildings. They left only the mission church. Workers built a large church next to it in 1876. The mission church became part of the city.

In 1906, an earthquake shook San Francisco. A fire swept through the city. Many buildings in San Francisco were ruined. The church next to San Francisco de Asís fell. But the little adobe church of San Francisco de Asís did not crumble or burn.

People began to call this area in the city the Mission District. The old mission church still stands in the Mission District. This mission is also called Mission Dolores.

People still attend religious services at the adobe church.

Mission Santa Clara lies within Santa Clara University.

MISSION SANTA CLARA DE ASÍS

In 1851, Jesuit priests took control of Mission Santa Clara de Asís. The Catholic priests used the mission as a college. Students came to take classes there. The college became a university in 1912.

College officials laid out the school grounds around the old mission. Workers repaired mission buildings. They fixed roofs and strengthened or replaced adobe walls with wood.

Remains of an adobe wall from the original mission (*right*) stand near the chapel and gardens at Santa Clara University.

The mission church burned down in 1926. Students, priests, and firefighters saved some objects. Workers built the new church to look just like the old one. Officials at Santa Clara hung the old mission bell in the new church in 1929.

MISSION SAN JOSÉ

An earthquake crumbled Mission San José in 1868. Only a small part of its quadrangle remained standing. In 1869, the priest in charge of the mission rebuilt the church. He constructed a church made of redwood over the old church floor.

Mission San José

A group decided to rebuild the mission church in 1982. They wanted the church to be just like the first one. Many others joined the building project. Workers moved the wooden church. Scientists searched the area and mission grounds for objects from the old mission. The objects were saved to be placed in the new church. Builders made the church walls of adobe. They used the old building methods. But they added steel to the walls to make them strong.

A priest held services to celebrate the new church on June 11, 1985. Father Fermín de Lasuén had founded Mission San José on that day 188 years earlier.

The interior of Mission San José was rebuilt to look as it did in the early 1800s.

San Rafael Arcángel was built anew in 1949.

MISSION SAN RAFAEL ARCÁNGEL

Mission San Rafael Arcángel stood empty from 1842 to 1855. People tore down some of the buildings. They wanted the adobe bricks, roof beams, and roof tiles for their own building projects.

Catholic priests returned to the mission in 1855. The mission was in poor condition. The priests decided to tear down the remaining mission buildings. Mission San Rafael Arcángel became the only mission to have all its buildings completely destroyed.

In 1949, people raised money to rebuild the mission church. The church has become a museum. At the museum, visitors can see old objects from the mission, such as paintings and tools.

A long porch runs alongside the simple adobe walls of Mission San Francisco Solano.

MISSION SAN FRANCISCO SOLANO

In the late 1800s, the Catholic Church sold San Francisco Solano. The new owner stored hay and wine in some mission buildings. The owner did not take care of the buildings.

The priests' rooms are the only areas left from the original mission buildings.

The Historical Landmarks League bought the mission in 1903. The group repaired some of the mission. But the 1906 San Francisco earthquake damaged many of the mission buildings. Work to restore the mission began again in 1911 and 1940. Church bells and other items from the first church were placed in the new mission.

The mission buildings are today part of Sonoma State Historic Park. Travelers can tour the mission grounds and church. At the mission site, visitors can see some of the priests' living areas.

BAY AREA NATIVE AMERICANS

More than half of the Native American population in the Bay Area died from sicknesses brought by the Spanish. Many feared that the Coast Miwok and Ohlone peoples had died out.

But people with Ohlone and Coast Miwok ancestors still live in the San Francisco Bay area. They are working hard to have their people and their history recognized. The two groups have asked for memorials to be placed at the five Bay Area missions. The memorials would honor American Indians who built, worked, and died at the missions. In the late 1990s, just such a memorial was placed at San Francisco Solano.

LAYOUTS

These diagrams of the San Francisco Bay area missions show what the missions look like in modern times. Modern-day missions may not look exactly like the original missions that the Spanish priests founded. But by studying them, we can get a sense of how neophytes and missionaries lived.

San Francisco de Asís:
This mission was founded on June 29, 1776. Its adobe chapel still stands in the city of San Francisco. People can attend special church services there.

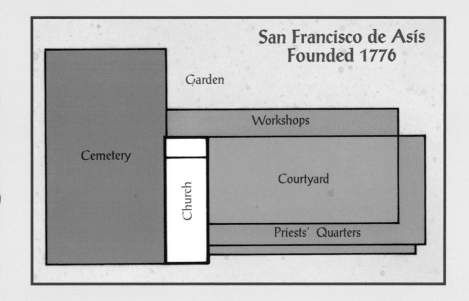

San Francisco de Asís
Founded 1776

Garden

Cemetery

Church

Workshops

Courtyard

Priests' Quarters

Santa Clara de Asís:

Founded in 1777, this mission was used as a private college from 1851 to 1912. The mission is still the center of Santa Clara University.

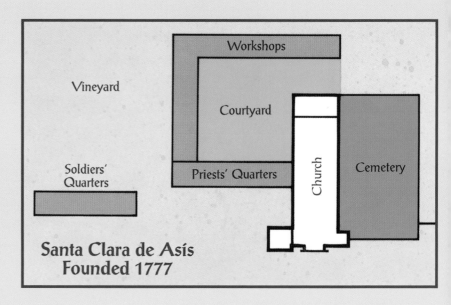

Santa Clara de Asís Founded 1777

Vineyard

Workshops

Courtyard

Priests' Quarters

Church

Cemetery

Soldiers' Quarters

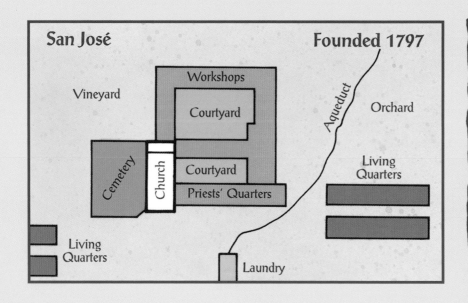

San José   **Founded 1797**

Vineyard

Workshops

Courtyard

Courtyard

Priests' Quarters

Cemetery

Church

Aqueduct

Orchard

Living Quarters

Living Quarters

Laundry

San José:

This mission was established on June 11, 1797. The neophyte Estanislao led a revolt against the mission in 1828. The mission chapel was rebuilt in the 1980s.

San Rafael Arcángel: Priests from San Francisco de Asís founded this mission as a hospital in 1817.

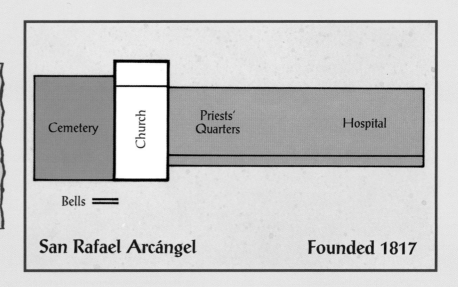

San Rafael Arcángel   Founded 1817

Cemetery | Church | Priests' Quarters | Hospital

Bells

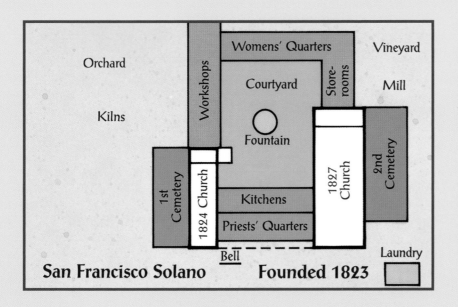

San Francisco Solano   Founded 1823

Orchard
Kilns
Workshops
Womens' Quarters
Vineyard
Courtyard
Storerooms
Mill
Fountain
1st Cemetery
1824 Church
1827 Church
2nd Cemetery
Kitchens
Priests' Quarters
Bell
Laundry

San Francisco Solano: This mission was established on July 4, 1823. San Francisco Solano was the last of the missions. It is currently part of a state park.

TIMELINE

1500s   Spanish and English explorers claim Alta California.

1769   San Diego de Alcalá becomes the first mission in Alta California.

1776   Anza expedition reaches San Francisco Bay area; settlers begin building the pueblo that becomes San Francisco and Mission San Francisco de Asís.

1777   Mission Santa Clara de Asís is founded.

1797   Mission San José is established.

1817   San Rafael Arcángel opens as a hospital.

1821   Mexico takes control of Alta California.

1823   San Francisco Solano is founded; it is the twenty-first and last mission.

1830s   The Mexican government begins to secularize the missions.

1846   The Mexican War between Mexico and the United States begins.

1848   The Mexican War ends; the United States gains control of California.

1850   California becomes the thirty-first state.

1850s   The U.S. government returns missions to the Catholic Church.

1890s   Mission restorations begin; the work continues through present times.

GLOSSARY

adobe: bricks made by mixing clay soil, sand, water, and straw. Workers dried and hardened the bricks by placing them under the sun.

Alta California: the old Spanish name for the modern-day state of California

Californios: the Spanish word for the early settlers of Alta California

missionaries: teachers sent out by religious groups to spread their religions to others

missions: centers where religious teachers work to spread their beliefs to others

neophytes: in Alta California, Native Americans who have joined the Roman Catholic faith and community

presidios: Spanish forts for housing soldiers

pueblos: towns

quadrangle: an area or patio surrounded by buildings on four sides

rancho: ranch. Californios used mission land to create ranches.

reservations: areas of land the U.S. government set aside for Native Americans

secularize: to change from religious to nonreligious. The missions were secularized when the Mexican government took control of mission lands from Spanish priests.

smallpox: a serious illness that spread easily and caused high fevers and blisters. This disease was carried to the Americas from Europe and killed thousands of Native Americans.

tule: a reed that grows in North American marshes

PRONUNCIATION GUIDE*

Anza, Juan Bautista de	AHN-sah, WAHN baw-TEES-tah day
El Camino Reál	el kah-MEE-no ray-AHL
Estanislao	ays-tah-nees-LAOW
Lasuén, Fermín Francisco de	lah-soo-AYN, fair-MEEN frahn-SEES-koh day
Miwok	MEE-wahk
Ohlone	oh-LOH-nee
Pico, Pío	PEE-koh, PEE-oh
San Francisco de Asís	SAHN frahn-SEES-koh day ah-SEES
San Francisco Solano	SAHN frahn-SEES-koh soh-LAHN-no
San José	SAHN hoh-SAY
San Rafael Arcángel	SAHN rah-fah-AYL ahrk-AHN-hayl
Santa Clara de Asís	SAHN-tah KLAH-rah day ah-SEES
Serra, Junípero	SEH-rrah, hoo-NEE-pay-roh
Vallejo, Mariano Guadalupe	vah-YAY-hoh, mah-ree-AH-noh (g)wah-dah-LOO-pay

* Local pronunciations may differ.

TO LEARN MORE

Abbink, Emily. *Monterey Bay Area Missions.* Minneapolis: Lerner Publications Company, 2008. Learn more about the other missions in northern California.

California Missions Resource Center http://www.missionscalifornia.com This site offers online slideshows of California missions, timelines, and interactive maps.

Mission San Francisco de Asís (Mission Dolores) http://www.virtuar.com/ysf2/dolores .htm Visitors to this page can find images and take a virtual tour of the first mission founded in the San Francisco Bay area.

Mission San Francisco de Solano http://www.parks.ca.gov/pages/479/ files/missionsfsolano.htm This California State Parks Web page presents a virtual tour of Mission Solano and its grounds.

Mission Santa Clara de Asís http://www.scu.edu/visitors/mission Visitors can view images of the mission church located on the campus of Santa Clara University.

Nelson, Libby, and Kari A. Cornell. *California Missions Projects and Layouts.* Minneapolis: Lerner Publications Company, 2008. This book provides guides on how to build models of a mission. It also offers layouts of California's twenty-one missions.

Twenty-One California Missions http://www.ca-missions.org/ contact.html This website features links to official Web pages, images, and virtual tours of the missions in California.

INDEX